College is an expensive necessity for the 21st Century worker. Besides a home, college is probably one of the most expensive purchases a buyer will make in their lifetime. College buyers are making this significant purchase when they are younger, less financially experienced, and extremely optimistic about their future prospects. If those prospects come true, the student is launched on their way to a great life. If the student buyer guesses wrong, they could be mired in a lifetime of debt.

The student loan crisis is a testament to how many buyers guess wrong. Forty-eight million borrowers owe more than $1.5 Trillion dollars in student loan debt. Student loan debt now exceeds both automobile debt and credit card debt. My work in this field has been with college buyers that guessed wrong. I am a student loan debt repayment expert. I have worked with thousands of college students and their parents across the US to help them get affordable student loan payments.

My work is a logical extension to the work done by Dan Evertsz to ensure that students make the best and most optimal choice in the first place. We have worked together many times. But, it is still true that an ounce of prevention is worth a pound of cure. The tips in this book are the quintessential "ounces of prevention".

It is hard for families to know everything that they need to know. That makes the college cost battle an asymmetric war. Read this book so that you can be better prepared to ensure that you maximize your investment in college and minimize the amount of debt that you take. I am thrilled that Dan has collected the tips that he offers daily and put them in a book.

Ce Cole Dillon
Author, What You Don't Know About Student Loans Can Hurt You (Don't Finance What You Can Afford)

AF887390

20 STUPID MISTAKES PARENTS MAKE WHEN APPLYING FOR COLLEGE FUNDING

Dan Evertsz
The College Money Pro

Foreword by Gerna Benz

WI Publish

20 Stupid Mistakes Parents Make When Applying for College Funding

www.collegemoneypros.com

WI Publish

WIPublish
A Division of Women Ignite International, Boise, ID
www.womenigniteinternational.com

Certain names have been changed upon request.

Printed in the United States of America

TABLE OF CONTENTS

Mistake #9: Only applying to schools in your home state.

Mistake #10: Having your student concentrate on their major instead of their career.

Mistake #11: Not calculating your student's Return on Investment.

Mistake #12: Assuming middle and upper-middle class parents won't be eligible for financial aid because they have equity in their home and make up to $1,000,000 per year.

Mistake #13: Focusing your time and energy solely on private scholarships instead of trying to learn strategies to access and maximize aid from other sources.

Mistake #14: Wrongly assuming only minority students, athletes, and exceptionally gifted students get financial aid and merit scholarships.

Mistake #15: Not monitoring your student's social media.

Mistake #16: Assuming all schools are created equal and will be able to give you the same amounts of money.

Mistake #17: Assuming it doesn't matter where you keep your money because it is all counted the same way.

Mistake #18: My certified public accountant (CPA) or tax preparer is familiar and qualified to fill out financial aid forms -- I'll let him/her do it.

Mistake #19: Waiting until January (or even worse, after January) of your child's senior year of high school, to start working on your college financial aid planning. My financial planner understands late stage college planning.

Mistake #20: Going through the financial aid process by yourself because it's "cheaper".

Conclusion. Now What?

About Dan Evertsz

DEDICATION

This book is dedicated to my wife, Deborah, and my two beautiful children, Ashlee and Khari, whose unconditional love and support have provided me the desire and inspiration to complete this project.

ACKNOWLEDGEMENTS

In the pursuit of completing this book, it became clear that this project was going to be difficult to complete independently. An incredibly blessed life that keeps me running from meetings to speaking engagements, volunteering for non-profit events and high school football games; it's been very tough to complete the writing of this book.

I want to acknowledge my sales coach, Eric Lofholm. I joined his "Guaranteed Results Coaching Program, which has pushed me to operate at a level 10 at all times. It has provided me a blueprint to get things done on a daily basis. I probably would still be working on mistake number 10 if Eric hadn't encouraged me to finish the book yesterday. I rolled up my sleeves and spent countless hours discussing this book and collaborating with my college planning colleagues. Many of them were unaware of how helpful they were but I really appreciate their assistance.

I want to especially thank Mr. Gerna Benz of Bay College Planning, who started this journey with me back in 2005. I can still remember our first workshop where we were sweating profusely during our first presentation in a room full of parents. We were brand new in the business and did not have a clue how complicated this process could be. The demand for help was very high, and as a result, clients signed up after that first presentation. Fast forward twelve years and we are both nationally known experts in the college planning arena.

I want to thank my wife again for her constant positive attitude and support. She has been my rock for the past 26 years. I feel very blessed to have her as my best friend.

FOREWORD

It's important to have a plan to pay for college. College loan debt is ranked second in all consumer debt, second only to mortgages. The outstanding student loan debt is nearly $1.3 trillion and continues to grow. There are 7 million borrowers that are currently in default on their student loans. The importance of knowing these figures is to help motivate parents and students to learn proactive strategies that they can employ in their own college planning endeavors. For over 11 years, we have been teaching parents that in choosing a best-fit college for your student, everything is related to everything. This mantra means - depending on the academic merit of your student will determine the possible admission to a school, which will determine the possibility of scholarship consideration, which will determine the final gap in the cost of attendance a parent will need to pay to send their student to that school.

The most important piece in solving the cost for the college puzzle is to "know your number". Parents can use multiple resources in determining what their number is. When we refer to "knowing your number", we are referring to a family's Expected Family Contribution (EFC) which is a dollar index the government imposes based on the income and asset valuations of the family household. A family's financial profile has a huge impact on what schools they should consider.

As the proud parent of two girls (Kara and Kiely), one in college and one in high school, I know the difficulty parents face when navigating the college planning and funding process. Understanding your numbers and the true cost of colleges will help your family lower your overall cost of college. You will be empowered and not in fear of the college planning process!

Gerna Benz
CEO, Bay College Planning
San Ramon, California

INTRODUCTION

Before I delve into my introduction, I want to explain the title of this book. My purpose is not to insult parents, but to encourage you to take action and not procrastinate in preparing for the largest financial obligation (other than the purchase of your home) your family will probably face.

I've been working in the field of college planning since 2005, helping families navigate the complicated maze of funding college in a comfortable manner without breaking the bank. However, college planning is more than funding and includes families in all aspects of the process. Over the years, I have spoken to thousands of families across the country. I'm happy to say I've acquired the knowledge to develop college planning and funding plans for families who are often told they make too much money to receive financial assistance for college. They are called the middle class, the one's that seem to always get screwed. Fast forward to 2017, we just signed up family number 913 to our parent membership program.

This book is intended to help educate parents of college-bound students to avoid the many mistakes parents make when applying for college funding. By avoiding these common mistakes, parents will have a much better way of maintaining their current lifestyle without jeopardizing their future retirement.

For the past 20 years, the cost of a college education has increased at least twice the rate of inflation. Parents are not prepared to pay $100,000 plus for a four-year education. God forbid if a family has multiple children! I was recently doing a financial assessment of a family with three children. Based on estimates at the schools they intend to apply to, the cost for that family exceeds $350,000. This expenditure will happen within a short period of time.

This book will allow you to understand what's needed to avoid many sleepless nights parents may have when the reality of this overwhelming expense comes close to reality. I will show you strategies that can be employed to rest easy at night. Every family must understand the tools that can make a college education an affordable reality.

MISTAKE #1

Not doing research to understand financial aid and merit scholarship formulas.

Reality: Every family should understand how to and apply for financial aid, which is solely awarded on "financial need" and is calculated by using the cost of attendance at a school and subtracting the Expected Family Contribution (EFC). The EFC is calculated by completing the Free Application for Student Aid, otherwise known as FAFSA. It is the number the government has determined your family can afford to pay (based on your income), the number of people in your family, your assets, and your child's income and assets. The difference after you subtract these two numbers is your "financial need" or eligibility for financial aid. If you haven't noticed, this has nothing to do with a student's ethnic background or athletic ability. Financial Aid is based solely on a federal formula:

COA (Cost of Attendance) - EFC (Expected Family Contribution) = FN (Financial Need)

As a college planning and funding expert, I have helped many six-figure families access thousands of dollars of financial aid. These families came to my office and informed me that there is no way they could qualify and only expected to be offered loans. Fast forward to their child's senior year and they are now eligible to receive financial aid. Did you know that there are over 600 schools across the country that will help families who make up to $170,000 per year receive financial aid? That number won't be as high as a family that makes

$100,000 per year, but I believe that every little bit helps in this very expensive endeavor.

Merit Scholarships: Many colleges and universities will offer merit scholarships to families with students who have several accomplishments. These schools take into consideration a student's grade point average, ACT or SAT test scores, as well as a student's involvement in community service, leadership, internships, sports, and volunteering. These qualities can lead to substantial scholarships, commonly known as merit scholarships. These are awarded regardless of a family's income level. Attaining these accomplishments should begin as early as a student's freshman year in high school.

Case Study: The Brown family has a pool cleaning business, and the wife is employed by the city they reside in. The student had a 3.7 GPA, tested well on the SAT, and was involved in many school activities. The family's adjusted gross income is $140,000. After examining their budget and cash flow, we determined their tax professional was doing them an injustice by omitting many legal write-offs on their 1040 tax returns. After review by our CPA, who specializes in college planning, their adjusted income was reduced to less than $95,000, which qualified their child for a $9,000 state grant, as well as an additional $30,000 of aid from the college she enrolled at. Their net cost to attend the $60,000 institution was $21,000 per year, which was less than the state school, which had a cost of attendance of $25,000, with no aid.

MISTAKE # 2

Procrastinating to start the process until your student's senior year.

Reality: This is easily avoidable. Every year I have families that contact me in their student's senior year and say, "My kid is a senior, and I need help trying to figure out this process. Many of these families have seen me present and speak during one of my educational workshops, which makes it frustrating because if the family had started the process a year earlier, we could have saved them thousands of dollars.

Case Study: The Jones family came in for an assessment in January of their student's senior year. The student has a cumulative academic GPA of 2.9. In their state of residence, there is a state grant that will pay 100% of the student's tuition. In order to qualify, the parents need to have an adjusted gross income of less than $95,000 per year for a family of five, which they have. The other qualification is a cumulative academic GPA of 3.0. As a college planning professional, we mentor students to achieve the highest grades based on effort. We have helped many students increase their grades substantially. By starting late in the process, the family has lost free tuition of approximately $8,000 per year, or a total of $40,000 (most students graduate in 5 or 6 years at state schools).

MISTAKE #3

Assuming the cost and process of college admissions are the same as when they (the parents) went to college.

Reality: In the society we live in today, most parents are consumed by the daily rigors of work and family activities. Time flies so fast that it is very easy to look up and see our lovely children having blossomed into fine young adults—a step closer to college and the real world. As a parent of two children, one attending a university and the other in high school, I find myself wondering where the time has gone. My kids are no longer young children, but close to experiencing the reality of the society we live in. Before I attended college, I made my list of schools and applied, and was accepted to most of the schools. However, times have changed. Since 2006, the senior class at high schools throughout the country are the largest in history. As a result, there are more students vying for admission to colleges. I reside in the state of California. There are numerous schools throughout this very heavily populated and popular state. As a result, over 70% of high school students in my state remain here for college. This has resulted in impacted schools with more applicants than spots available. In addition, most classes are filled to capacity, so some students are unable to register for classes needed in order to progress to the next year. Additionally, being a legacy at state sponsored schools is no longer considered in the application process. At private universities, legacy continues to be a factor, but many families cannot afford the higher prices unless they understand the merit scholarship process and history of funding at private schools.

As a result, families should apply to a minimum of ten schools to have a chance for admittance to a few schools of their choice. My suggestion is to do your research and start the process early. Did you know that the majority of schools only post their school's 6-year graduation rates? You need to know the 4-year graduation rate before accepting your final choice school. Remember 2 extra years can cost a family $50,000 plus. You don't want that to be you.

Case Study: In 2005, I was the typical middle-class parent working hard to support my family with very limited time for outside activities. Although my daughter was consistently bugging me to do this and that, my schedule didn't allow for much involvement on my part.

If I only knew what I know now, my bank account would have quite a few more zeros in it. My daughter only applied to four schools, and two of them cost over $50,000 per year. I didn't discover this until I took the time to visit their websites. Remember, kids don't pay attention to the cost of college! They just know they want to apply to a particular school based on peer pressure, sports, parents, or marketing. In some cases, they are recruited because they are academically talented. You may wonder why you are receiving all this mail from schools across the country. Students who have scored high on either the PSAT or have taken the SAT or ACT are being tracked by schools that have paid for this information.

My daughter was a good student in high school. No, she did not have a 4.0 GPA, but she was somewhere near 3.5 to 3.7. When I visited the websites of the two finalists, I discovered her favorite school cost over $50,000 a year. I quickly informed her that a competing school (Howard University) fit my budget, and that is the university we needed to concentrate on. What I didn't know was she qualified for an in-house scholarship that would have reduced the cost of attendance to less than what I paid at Howard. FYI, you don't know what you don't know.

MISTAKE #4

Having your student take the lead without parents being involved in the process.

Reality: This is a huge mistake I often hear about when it is much too late. Many students do not take the cost of a four-year school into consideration, much less 6-year graduation averages. Most get their information from peers at school. I have come across high schools with very uplifting and dedicated guidance counselors. Unfortunately, some schools and, therefore, students are not provided with similar guidance. Many counselors tend to be overworked and under compensated. At public schools in California, the average counselor has 60 to 900 students they are responsible for. I'll go into this in more detail in Mistake # 5.

In the college admissions arena, there are three types of admission applications:

1. Early decision. If your student applies to a college under early decision and that college accepts the student, it is considered a contract and the student must attend that particular school. For this reason, I DO NOT recommend applying early decision.

2. Early action. When the student applies, he/she will have preferential treatment and acceptance into schools that participate in this process.

3. Regular admission. This is the last admission instrument.

Case Study: Mrs. Adair was referred to me by one of my clients. She began our conversation by explaining that she only needed limited help. She was boasting about her daughter, saying she is a hard worker and is to be applauded. She also proudly stated that she allowed her daughter to take the reins of the application and funding process. As she spoke, I couldn't help but wonder, "If your daughter has done everything so well, then why are you in need?" She told me about the schools that her daughter was accepted into, and I congratulated her on a job well done.

However, I knew there was more to this story. As the conversation continued, she disclosed that her daughter applied for early decision and was accepted. Afterwards, they were offered merit scholarships of up to $20,000 at another school she applied to. However, the highly rated school in Boston, that she now is required to attend, offered no money. This family made a huge mistake that is going to cost them $80,000-$100,000 over the next four years. Doing simple research or contacting a college planning professional would have made a huge financial difference for this family.

MISTAKE #5

Relying solely on your high school guidance counselor's advice.

Reality: I want to clarify that this mistake is not meant to demean or belittle the importance of a good high school guidance counselor. However, I have encountered various counselors and questioned their intentions. In every field, you will find people who are excellent at their profession, and people who are not. As stated earlier, most high school guidance counselors are overworked and underpaid. I really don't know how they succeed, especially in public schools across the nation where the ratio of counselor to student is overwhelmingly disproportionate. With that said, as a college funding professional who has had many interactions with guidance counselors, I have noticed that the majority of them know very little about funding for college. Although they may do a great job of getting kids into college, families want to know how they can reduce the out-of-pocket cost of a college education. That is where professionals in this industry, commonly known as college planners, can really help.

The first thing a family needs to know is whether or not the college or university has a history of providing maximum financial aid and/or scholarships. Personally, I would call the financial aid office and inquire about their generosity of helping working families. Some schools will flat-out tell you if they rely mainly on loans, or that they don't provide merit scholarships if you're not eligible for financial aid. Again, starting this process early and doing the research can save your family thousands of dollars. As previously noted, I've come in contact with some very good high school college guidance counselors who go above and beyond to help families and their college-bound students. It seems that if students get more involved with their teachers and/or counselor, he or she will step up and go the extra mile. However, unless your student asks the right questions, this may not happen and that's when you as a parent need to get involved.

Quick tip: Have your student call the school as opposed to you because it demonstrates leadership and independence. Some schools will note that on their file. Remember, when your student arrives at college, you will not be there. The more they are prepared, the better.

MISTAKE #6

Getting the bulk of your information from your WCB (water cooler buddy at work).

Reality: Where do most parents get their information about college funding? Many, but not all parents, get their information from co-workers and other parents. These can be some of your options for gathering information, but it should not be your only resource. Don't get me wrong, there are some very well-informed parents who have been through this process. However, what's good for that family at that particular school is not necessarily the same for your family.

Remember earlier when I spoke about understanding the financial aid and merit scholarship arena? Your child and that family's child most likely do not have the same grades or similar scores on the SAT or ACT. Returning to the financial aid formula, your family's income and assets may be very different than that of your friends. Often, people speak in generalities and parents don't always disclose the entire story.

Quick Tip: It is not wise to only rely on advice from people at work or friends who have gone through this process. While some advice is better than no advice, it's impossible to compare your friend's or co-worker's experience to your family. I'm sure you've heard the saying "never compare apples and oranges". The same goes with college planning. There is a right set of schools for your student that may not be a good fit for your friend's child who has totally different thoughts and ideas on school selection.

A very common phrase that I hear from parents is that their friend's child got a full ride from "College A". I then begin asking questions: What is their family's EFC (Expected Family Contribution)? What is their child's GPA? What is their child's SAT/ACT test score? What is their potential major? How large is the school they attended? Was the school public or private? I could go on and on with several more comparisons. The bottom line is there are many variables in college planning. Once you peel back the outside layer and really dig in, you will find out what's really under the skin.

MISTAKE #7

Waiting to apply for college admission until the deadline.

Reality: Students in our program have a very busy summer before entering their senior year in high school. During that time, their personal statement essay will be been completed with the help of our coach. Our essay coach does not write essays for our students but helps to bring out their passions on paper. Additionally, they are studying for the SAT and ACT. By October, they have attended our college admissions boot camp. This boot camp is specifically designed to coach our students on how and when to complete their college applications. I'm a big believer in the early bird catches the worm. At many schools, applying for early admission shows a more responsible student than one who waits until the deadline to apply.

Case Study: I recently received a call from a parent in my program. They had attended a local college fair with schools from across the country in attendance. The parent and student were informed by her number one school that the application deadline had passed. I was under the impression that the student applied right after the boot camp, but she procrastinated and used the information from the Common App, which stated the school's deadline to be a month from now. Luckily, they followed my advice and applied to 10 schools and the student has already been accepted to six of them.

Parents, please do not let your children run the show when it comes to this process. I know how busy we are as parents but try to be as involved as possible. I hate to get that phone call where I hear the student in the background shedding tears because they didn't follow instructions.

MISTAKE #8

Being too busy to attend college fairs at your child's school.

Reality: Many colleges across the country participate in college fairs targeting college-bound students. These college fairs are often held at local high schools or at non-profit organizations, such as churches. I realize that the lines at many of these fairs can be long. However, the information that you and your student will obtain from schools is invaluable. Some schools may even offer on-site admissions. I speak annually at a large college fair at the Los Angeles Convention Center that typically has 10,000 people in attendance. These college fairs often have information-packed breakout sessions featuring different experts on various topics.

Information is crucial for you and your student. The person hosting the school's booth may be the admissions officer or head of admissions. As previously stated, admittance to college is very competitive. You will learn tips to help your child get accepted to the school of their choice. Any family with a college bound student needs to have complete involvement and educate themselves about this process. Check with your high school guidance counselor to ensure you have college fair dates on your calendar.

Case Study: Information from the source is king. Learning should be continual in anyone's life, regardless of what you do as a career. As a college planning professional who has studied this subject for thousands of hours, I'm near the top of my game when it comes to this subject. However, I know many people in different professions who are so full of themselves that they think they know everything. I'm sure you know a few of these people as well.

Throughout the Fall and Spring, there are several college fairs that come through each area of the country. Many times, they will come directly to your student's high school. I try my best to attend at least two per year. Invariably, every time I attend a college fair I come away learning something new to help the families that are in my membership. Four years ago, I attended a workshop at St. Mary's College in Orinda, California (a great private school with good merit that is a suburb of Oakland, California). I noticed a school that was touting their nursing program. I stood in line like everyone else to learn more. To my surprise, one of the people manning the table was the Director of Admissions for the University of Tampa. When I told her about my program, we set up a time to chat about the school's nursing program. This is a hidden gem located in downtown Tampa. The cost of the school was affordable, and their nursing program was top of the line. Historically, 90% of the students who graduate from this program passed the State exams on the first try. Best of all, they covered a high percentage of need as well as good merit scholarships for middle-class families. I have recommended them to many of my students who are going into nursing to apply and see what happens.

A quick tip for parents and their students: Ask every school what percentage of need they cover and what are the qualifications are. If the person can't answer, find out who can and follow up. Keep notes on every school you speak with and try to sit down and rate the school. Most families pick up the brochures and stuff them in a large bag provided by one of the advertisers. This is a key and common mistake many students and parents make every year. Also, don't just visit the booths of the schools you are familiar with, check out the schools you may never heard of. You may get lucky like I did.

MISTAKE #9

Only applying to schools in your home state.

Reality: We highly encourage students to apply to schools out of state, especially if you live in a state that is heavily populated. The reason for this is that mini-schools and the less populated states may offer incentives to get your student to attend their college. This is a strategy that every family should employ if they have a child who they feel is mature enough to live away from home.

If you happen to reside in the Western United States, there is an exchange agreement called Western Undergraduate Exchange which is an agreement between California and 11 neighboring states that provides a significant discount to families that would normally pay double tuition for out-of-state tuition. In addition, if you have a higher achieving student, you may also receive merit scholarships which will reduce your family's out-of-pocket expenses.

In my program, I have a student who was awarded a full tuition scholarship to a school in a neighboring state, with most expenses paid (i.e. tuition, travel, books, computer, fees), with the exception of room and board. His parents are ecstatic. They were expecting to pay approximately $40,000 for his college education; however, I knew the background of the student and suggested they apply at that particular school. My advice will save them $110,000 over four years.

Quick Tip: Many parents are not comfortable with their student leaving home and venturing to a distant state for college. Heck, my wife doesn't want my son to go to college more than 50 miles from home. As far as I'm concerned, he can go across the country. My son needs to grow and not be pampered by his mom all the time. (She is going to kill me when she reads this!)

You know your kids better than anyone. Some students in my program should not venture far from home because of their lack of maturity. I get it. If they are mature, don't hold them back if they want to venture away from home. If they don't need to cross the country, let them attend college in a neighboring state. One of the best ways to instill independence in your student is to let them be independent and make their own mistakes and learn from them. It's amazing how many kids go away for college and return after one year almost a different person because they have matured so much. They are still that great child that you raised, but their perspectives on life will probably be different. I see this in students that I haven't spoken with in years that hit me up on social media all the time. It's great to know you had a little something to do with the young person who is successful out in the business world. This is why I love this business. I feel so good when we reopen the lines of communication on a totally different level. WOW!

MISTAKE #10

Having your student concentrate on their major instead of their career.

The normal practice for many students is to first choose a school, then decide on a major that sounds interesting. Many students do not put serious time into selecting the career that they may be gainfully employed in for the next 40 to 50 years.

Reality: The correct sequence should be to do an assessment in order to determine best-fit careers, then determine the major that corresponds with their career choice. Once the student has an idea of three or four career choices, they should begin researching the schools that fit their long-term objective.

Did you know that over 50% of college students end up changing their major while in college? Often, students mature and realize the impact of their career choice. Although it is understandable that a young adult is not 100% sure of their future career, I feel that changing one's major can be a regrettable mistake. Choosing the wrong major can increase your family's cost of a college education if your student takes six months to a year break from school figuring out their career path. There are great resources out there, such as the Birkman Assessment. This assessment measures 70 internal markers to help students with this process. Although it is costly, if you put time and attention into this area, it will financially reward you and your family for many years.

Case Study: You should concentrate on your career instead of your major. The normal practice for many students is first to choose a school, then decide on a major that sounds interesting. Many students do not put serious thought into the career that they may be gainfully employed in for the next 40 to 50 years. Reality: The correct sequence should be to do an assessment in order to determine best-fit careers, then determine the major that corresponds with their career choice. Once the student has an idea of three or four career choices, they should begin researching the schools that fit their long-term objective.

Did you know that over 50% of college students end up changing their major while in college? Often, students mature and realize the impact of their career choice. Although it is understandable that a young adult is not 100% sure of their future career, I feel that changing one's major is regrettable but better to make that mistake now. I know many professionals in varied professions who hate their jobs. Many went into the wrong major based on what their parents wanted, not what they wanted. Choosing the wrong major can increase your family's college education costs if your student takes a six month to one- year break from school to figure out their career path.

There are great resources out there, such as the Birkman Assessment. This assessment measures seventy internal markers to help students with this process. Although it is costly, if you put time and attention into this area, it will financially reward you and your family for many years.

Does the current educational system really prepare your student for the real world? In most cases no, especially for high school students. I had a conversation with clients who have a daughter who has grown up in private boarding schools throughout high school and beyond. My clients are both professionals. Like every parent out there, we all want the best for our children. Since the 9th grade, they have invested over $400,000 in their student's high school and college education. She graduated from Pepperdine in Los Angeles and started her business career with a great salary in the human resources field. After being employed in that field for over a year, she confessed to her parents that she hated the field and quit her job. After trying a couple of other short careers, she found a love for catering and is now very happy running a food service department for a well-known store in the food services industry. Yikes, that was a ton of money spent to end up in the catering business! But you know what, she absolutely loves what she does for a living. That is the most important lesson for any student to discover what they really want to do for a living. Now it's not a job, it something you love and look forward to your work day.

Another perfect example is from my own daughter. Her life's dream growing up was to work with animals and become a Veterinarian. She entered college as a Biology major. I remember getting a call during her junior year. Because I know her so well, I knew something was wrong by the tone of her voice. She tells me that she has been speaking with graduate students in the Veterinary field of study. She asked, "Dad, did you know that graduate students in the Veterinary field need to go to graduate school for six more years?" My response was, "Don't you remember this conversation when you were a senior in high school?" "Yeah, but I really wasn't paying that much attention..." As a parent, these kids can blow us off in a minute.

Ashlee then informed me that she had been talking with her advisor at school, and she would like to stay in the health field and become a nurse. One huge problem—she will need to do an additional year of college to get her nursing degree. WOW! There goes another $30,000 expense I wasn't counting on. I gave her the okay, and guess what? She graduates and then informs me that she doesn't want to go directly to graduate school. Why? Because she isn't entirely sure she wants to be a nurse. My response was, "You are a grown woman and on your own to make your decisions. I'm done."

Fast forward three years later. I got a call from Ashlee, and she tells me that she is ready to go to graduate school. She says, "Dad, it's no fun struggling financially at $40,000-$50,000 per year in Washington D.C." Best of all, she has found a career that she absolutely loves. She did volunteer work at a local hospital in D.C. helping people get their lives back from all types of injuries both physical and mentally. It's been a long haul, but my daughter received her Master's in Occupational Therapy from NYU in New York. Yes, out of my wallet forever. It never ends. Now it's her brother's turn. He just graduated from high school. Please pray for me.

Career assessment, career assessment and again, career assessment. As stated earlier, the Birkman assessment is top of the line. There are many others career assessments available as well. Please spend time on this as you want your college investment to go toward a happy and fruitful career for your student.

MISTAKE #11

Not calculating your student's Return on Investment.

What is your student's Return on Investment (ROI) if he or she attends four-year university? Do you know the ROI at a public school versus a private school?

Reality: Have you ever taken the time to calculate your ROI if your child decides to attend community college for two years and then transfer to a four-year institution? These are questions many families never think about. However, as a parent and professional, this is something I think about all the time. We all want our kids to be successful, but how long will it take for us to recoup our investment? That's why I spoke earlier about choosing the correct career that's going to compensate your student when they enter the real world.

Case Study: My daughter is in graduate school at NYU. Our total cost for graduate studies is $240,000. My daughter will graduate and become an occupational therapist starting at approximately $80,000 per year. $80,000 x 3 =$240,000. It will take 3 years to recoup our return on investment. If she would only give us back that $240,000, I would really be the happiest man in the world. If you believe that's going to happen, I have a bridge that I want to sell to you (The Golden Gate Bridge).

MISTAKE #12

Assuming middle and upper-middle class parents won't be eligible for financial aid because they have equity in their home and make up to $1,000,000 per year.

Reality: Most families with income ranging from $75,000 - $600,000 per year are eligible for some form of financial aid. There is over $30 billion available each year from the Federal Government, states, colleges and universities, private foundations, and organizations. You just have to know how to get your "fair share". Unfortunately, most parents give up before they begin and assume they won't be eligible. This is exactly what the government and schools hope you will do so they can withhold more of these funds. Don't make this mistake! If you fall into this category, make sure you apply.

Although most financial aid is based on “need,” it is also important to remember that there is another category--in house college scholarships based on grades, test scores and community service. Many schools across the country are trying to attract these types of students. How do they do that? The offer free money to attract that profile student, regardless of the income and assets of their parents. If your student is academically on top of their “A” game, one of the primary scholarships awarded based on academic merit is the National Merit Scholarship Program. It is given to students who do extremely well on their PSAT/NMSQT scores. In addition, many schools (outside of the Ivy League) try to attract top students away from the more highly rated schools by offering academic scholarships. If your child is academically gifted, use this as a bargaining chip.

Quick Tip: Start the SAT prep process prior to the students taking the PSAT in their junior or sophomore year in high school. Step up to the plate and make an investment in a good SAT prep program before taking the PSAT. I've had several students that have followed my instructions and have attained National Merit Semi-Finalist status. Do you know what that means? Because of you our student's high score, he/she will receive up to 14 full ride offers from schools across the country. Think of it like this, investing $500 to $1,000 into a good course can provide returns up to $200,000. What a deal!

MISTAKE #13

Focusing your time and energy solely on private scholarships instead of trying to learn strategies to access and maximize aid from other sources.

Reality: Private scholarships make up only 2% of the money available to help pay for your child's college education. The other 98% comes from the Federal Government, the state that you live in, and the colleges and universities your child is applying to. Do your research. Historically, every school provides different amounts of free money.

There are billions of dollars available in private scholarships. However, this can be a long and tedious process. Start applying for scholarships when your student starts high school. Many scholarships will bank the money until your student starts college. Be very proactive and apply for at least 50 scholarships per month and you may be awarded up to $1,000 monthly.

Quick Tip: Have your student go to the counseling office and apply for the local scholarships which will have much less competition than private scholarships.

Case Study: As I mentioned earlier, parents who are on a search for scholarships should apply for up to 50 scholarships per month. This is rarely reality, but it can be if you and your student are determined to get free money via scholarships. I give this advice to every family in my membership, but most parents are too busy to stay on top of it. But for those of you who are serious and put in the time, there is over a billion dollars of scholarship money available that does not need to be repaid.

Over the past 12 years, I've had two families who took my advice. Guess what happened? They both received over $10,000 in outside scholarships. It can be done. Focus on applying to local scholarships (Rotary, Lions, Soroptimist, Fraternities and Sororities, etc.) Every company that you pay bills to monthly has a scholarship for both employees and customers. Check the company you work at. I guarantee that there is a high probability that they have a scholarship program. The money is out there. Don't let a couple of no's stop you. Do you know what no means? It means that you are getting closer to a yes.

MISTAKE #14

Wrongly assuming only minority students, athletes, and exceptionally gifted students get financial aid and merit scholarships.

Reality: Nothing could be further from the truth! "Need-based" financial aid is solely awarded on "financial need" which is calculated by taking the cost of attendance at a school and subtracting the family contribution, which is the amount of money the government assumes you can afford to pay based on your income, number of people in your family, assets, and your child's income and assets. After these two numbers are subtracted, the remainder is your "financial need" or eligibility for financial aid. If you haven't noticed, this has nothing to do with a student's ethnic background, athletic ability, or grades. It is purely based on a simple formula:

COA (Cost of Attendance) - FC (Family Contribution) = FN (Financial Need)

Quick Tips:

1. Academically Gifted Students – One of the primary scholarships awarded based on academic merit is the National Merit Scholarship Program. It is given to students who do extremely well on their PSAT/NMSQT scores. In addition, many schools (outside of the Ivy League) try to attract top students away from the more highly rated schools by offering academic scholarships. If your child is academically gifted, use this as a bargaining chip.

2. Athletes – Even if your child is not Division 1 sports material, do not assume that Division 2 or 3 schools will not offer you preferential packaging (more grants, less loans) to attract your child to their school. Make sure you get in touch with the athletic department and make it a point to meet the coach at each school you visit. In addition, get your student's high school coach to write letters of recommendation to each school.

3. Minorities – If your child is Black, Hispanic, or Native American, contact colleges and find out about the availability of scholarship programs for minorities. Although there is some debate over awarding these types of scholarships, colleges in 19 States currently make these types of awards.

4. For Self-Employed or Business Owners - If you currently own your own business or you are thinking of starting one, there are significant benefits when it comes to getting money for college. To begin with, business assets are counted less influentially than personal assets. In addition, you can control (or lower) your income during the years that your child is in college, thereby making you eligible for more financial aid. There are some good CPA's out there, but there are also some lazy CPA's who don't take advantage of all the write-offs you may be entitled to. We were able to find over $25,000 in write-offs for a client who owns a successful concrete contracting business. We encouraged him to amend the taxes which he did. The result was his daughter qualified for a state grant and received a financial aid package valued at $46,000 per year. Overall, owning or starting a business can be a big help in getting money for college.

MISTAKE #15

Not monitoring your student's social media.

Reality: Be very careful. Schools do check your student's FACEBOOK, INSTAGRAM, TWITTER, etc. Your child should be cautious when sharing pictures, posts, tweets, and videos. They may be at the wrong place (a friend's party) and "tag" themselves in photos after they visit a campus. It is not hard for an admissions representative to view a student's profiles. All students should check their privacy settings.

Case Study: Over the last 11 years, I've had two students who didn't take my advice seriously. One had an abundance of profanity on her page, and the other was in the background of a photo drinking beer with other students. Both had been admitted to their top choice school but were later denied admission after the school viewed their social media.

MISTAKE #16

Assuming all schools are created equal and will be able to give you the same amount of money.

Reality: All schools are not created equal and will not be able to give you the same financial aid package. Some schools receive a lot of money from alumni and corporations. These schools have more money to give out and are generally able to meet most or all of a student's financial need. Other schools, e.g. state universities, don't get private funds and rely solely on state and federal funds to help fill a student's financial need at their school. In many cases, these schools give them less money than families are eligible to receive. Therefore, it can end up costing more to send your child to a "cheaper" school if the university doesn't have the money to meet your need. It is very important that you know each school's history of giving money before you apply so that you're not blown away if you get a less than ideal financial aid package from your child's top school choice.

I am aware that many families don't have the time to do the research necessary to be successful at this task, however, the families that receive the most money are the ones who do their homework and start the process early. I strongly suggest doing as much as you can with the time you have.

Quick Tip: Doing research and discovering the hidden financial aid numbers and how they vary at different schools can be a real challenge. Every school is different. Some schools are open to providing you approximate numbers you may qualify for. This is happening more and more since I first joined the industry in 2005. Matter of fact, some schools have calculators on their websites that will provide the information. I still estimate that 70% of schools across the country do not provide this information on an individual basis. Check the schools you are thinking about applying to and try to find the information. Many school websites are saturated with so much information, it can be a real challenge to find the information you are looking for. Don't give up! It's there somewhere.

Personally, I would reach out to a college planning professional. We have software that can provide you with all the numbers at every school in the country. They will probably provide the information for at least one school without charging you for the information. That's what I would do, but everyone is different. Another great resource that may have the information is College Board. Your student probably has registered and has a user name and password. The website is free. There is a wealth of information they provide to students and parents. Just Google it.

MISTAKE #17

Assuming it doesn't matter where you keep your money because it is all counted the same way.

Reality: This is completely false. Where you keep your money could mean the difference between you getting $10,000 in financial aid (or much more) or receiving nothing at all! For example, money in the child's name is weighted much more heavily than money in the parent's name. If you don't know how to legally and ethically position your money properly for purposes of financial aid, you could end up losing thousands of dollars. Certain assets are counted much more heavily in the financial aid formula than others. For example, savings accounts, CD's, stocks, and bonds are all included and asked about on the FAFSA. However, it does NOT ask about the value of many alternative financial savings vehicles. If you have a financial planner, odds are your money is in some form in the stock market since they get paid a yearly percentage of your investments (commonly 1.0% to 1.3%).

As a late stage college planner, I applaud any family that has taken the incentive to save for college. I come in contact with an abundance of families that have saved little or nothing for one of the largest expenditures they will make.

Did you know that 529 college savings plans count against you in the FAFSA? A student asset will reduce aid eligibility by 20 percent of the net asset value. A portion of parents' assets are sheltered on the FAFSA, and the remaining assets are assessed on a bracketed system, reducing eligibility for need-based aid by at most

5.64% of the remaining unsheltered net asset value. College savings plans, however, have special treatment due to an amendment that became effective on July 1, 2009, that was enacted by the College Cost Reduction and Access Act of 2007. This legislation changed the treatment of college savings plans as assets and distributions.

Additional common savings vehicles were created under the Uniform Gift to Minors Act (UGMA) or its successor, the Uniform Transfer to Minors Act (UTMA). They are straightforward and inexpensive, however, there are considerable disadvantages to UGMA and UTMA accounts. My biggest concern is that UGMAs and UTMAs count against the student in the financial aid formula because they are assets. If you were financial aid eligible, you just lost 15% in potential financial aid. Assets in the parent's name count against 5.64% while assets in the students are assessed at 20%. Ouch! In addition, gifts made to an UGMA or UTMA account vests on the beneficiary. Once determined, neither the custodian nor the donor can change the beneficiary after the establishment of the account, and significantly, the custodian must deliver the balance of the account outright to the beneficiary when he or she reaches the age of majority (18 or 21, as defined by state law). That is a scary reality.

Coverdell Education Savings Accounts (ESAs) Education Savings Accounts, formerly Education IRAs, were of little significance until the passage of the Economic Growth and Tax Relief Reconciliation Act of 2001 (EGTRRA). EGTRRA increased the maximum annual contribution limit from $500 to $2,000 per beneficiary. A donor can make contributions to an ESA and a College Savings Plan for the same child in the same year. Many families are opting to send their children to private school. 529 plans are limited to paying for higher education. ESAs can be used to fund the primary and secondary school.

Quick Tip: The information contained in this chapter is information that a Licensed CPA or Financial Planner should have at their fingertips. Due to the many tax laws and changes in the codes in 2018, you should reach out to a local licensed professional in your area to clarify current information.

MISTAKE #18

My certified public accountant (CPA) or tax preparer is familiar and qualified to fill out financial aid forms -- I'll let him/her do it.

Reality: Unfortunately, CPAs and tax preparers are experts at tax planning and preparation, not financial aid planning. For example, a CPA or tax preparer might suggest that you put some or all of your assets in your child's name to save money on taxes. While this advice is well-meaning, it will usually kill your chances of getting financial aid. CPAs and tax preparers are not trained in filling out financial aid forms. In many cases, they will unknowingly complete these forms without understanding legal rules and regulations set forth by the Department of Education. If mistakes are made, you will have to re-submit these forms. It is likely that you will end up losing free money since it is awarded on a first come, first serve basis. Over the years, I have had many CPAs hire me to navigate the financial aid arena for their family. Most CPAs are pretty smart guys. Why would they hire me to help their family? You figure that one out.

Case Study: I have a family that I have been working with since the student was a sophomore in high school. The parents are separated and live apart from one another but still file their taxes jointly. The father lives in a rental home and the mom lives in their primary residence. Per guidelines of the Department of Education, the mother who is self-employed and has a low adjusted gross income, should be the parent to complete the FAFSA. My suggestion was to file "married, filing separately." The equity in a rental home does count against you in the financial aid formula. Although on their 1040s there was no rental income, the equity in the home disqualified them from a State grant of $13,000 of free money per year for four years. Their CPA couldn't understand why they needed the aid because he determined that it "wasn't necessary." Because of his stature as an experienced CPA, he would not pick up the phone and discuss why I suggested they file separately. This common mistake will cost the family over $50,000 of free money they should have received to lower their out-of-pocket cost of college. You don't know what you don't know.

MISTAKE #19

Waiting until January (or even worse, after January) of your child's senior year of high school, to start working on your college financial aid planning. My financial planner understands late stage college planning.

Reality: Since financial aid is based on your previous two years of income and assets, it is imperative to start your planning as soon as possible. If you want to legally position your income and assets to maximize your eligibility for financial aid, you must begin working on a plan at least two to three years in advance, preferably in your child's freshman or sophomore year. In reality, this should have started when your student was in grade school or younger. The longer you wait and the closer it gets to your child's senior year, the tougher it becomes to set up your financial picture without creating a "red flag" for the colleges and universities. It is important for you to know what your EFC is so you can prepare to start a college funding plan. Many parents start completing the FAFSA in October of their child's senior year. Let's assume you want to reposition your assets or shelter income property out of the financial aid formula. This won't help in during the senior year since the FAFSA now requires your 1040 tax returns two years prior to your student's last year in high school. My advice is if you haven't started planning, **DO IT NOW!**

Case Study: I can write about this chapter all day long, but you would get tired of me. Why? Because every single year I have people who hire me to help that should have come in a year or two earlier. I get so tired of hearing parents say, "We saw you speak two years ago. Our student is now a senior, and we need help."

People who have a plan and start early are the families that win the college money sweepstakes. The rules have changed in the last two years. Prior to 2016, Free Application for Federal Student Aid could not be completed until January of the student's senior year. The income and assets were based on an estimate of the base income year which is January 1 of the student's junior year through December 31 of the student's senior year. If they hadn't completed the FAFSA because they hadn't receive their W-2's or completed their tax returns, they would file based on an estimate and then go back into the system and make the changes once the tax forms were filed.

Well, that is all in the past now. The new system is based on your tax returns two years previous. If your student is graduating in the class of 2019, the FAFSA information you will provide will be from the 2017 tax returns. What happens if you have divorced or have been laid off after 2017? You will then to file an appeal with every school your kid applied to—a real pain in the you know what.

It gets worse. What if you own rental property that is disqualifying you from financial aid? You have no time to legally shelter your assets. Remember, there are a ton of loopholes in the Federal Financial Aid codes. We have families who have started early and with advice with their tax professionals, have saved thousands of dollars by starting the process in their child's sophomore year. This drives me crazy, but it is what it is. That is human nature. Bottom line—start the process and save thousands of dollars.

MISTAKE #20

Going through the financial aid process by yourself because it's "cheaper".

Reality: If this describes you, the colleges and Federal Government are going to love you! This allows them to maintain control over the process. It is crucial that parents understand how the process works and take back control. It always amazes me that people will readily use a doctor when they get sick, a lawyer when they get sued, but when they are going to send their child to college and spend between $20,000-60,000 per year, they want to do it themselves. If you are someone who has studied this subject for the last 5-10 years, you may have a good understanding of the financial aid process. However, without proper training to learn insider secrets and strategies, there is no way you are going to know how to access maximum money from each school. The moral of this story is "Don't Be Penny Wise and Pound Foolish!" Use an expert who can help you through this process and make sure you get everything you are entitled to.

Case Study: I'm a perfect example. When my daughter was a senior in high school, I made many of these same mistakes. I heard about the company that helped students and their parents access aid for college, but I didn't want to speak with them because, after all, I went to college, and it was a breeze. To be brutally honest, if I had to endure the rigid academic performance required today, I probably would have gone to community college. I was a good student that knew how to slide by and get decent grades. In today's world, that is not plausible, and I know my study habits would have resulted in much lower grades.

CONCLUSION. WHAT NOW?

Hopefully, you've received a few takeaways that can save your family thousands of dollars. Navigating the complicated maze of college planning and funding can be a real challenge. This complicated process is nothing like when our generation went to college. The process is constantly changing.

The reality of the cost of a college education should be discussed with all family members. Students need to know about financial literacy. The earlier families start this conversation, the better for your student, for they will surely operate with this knowledge when they leave your home. As I mentioned, this is constantly on my mind since I have a teenager who will be matriculating to college in the near future. As you know, it is very easy for teens to tune us out. I'm sure you understand what I'm talking about.

Don't give up and communicate with your teen until they understand. Guide them through this journey. One day you will hear, "Mom or Dad, you were right about many things you used to talk about." That might take a long time, but it will happen.

Understanding money and finances is only a part of maturity, but it surely helps in their personal growth. I am a big believer in being positive with our young adults. Remember, patience is a virtue. Education is the road to a successful life in the United States.

If you own any of these assets or find yourself in any of these situations, then you need our help:

■ Cash, stocks, mutual funds, bonds.
■ Equity in your home or you own a rental property or second home.
■ Insufficient or no plan to cover college costs for ALL your children.
■ Your child has no idea what he wants to do for a living.
■ Your child has no idea which major to select
■ Your child has chosen a major but has no idea what job prospects are available in his chosen field.
■ You have little or no desire to tackle this process on your own.

For more information, please visit here: http://collegemoneypros.com/webinar

Feel free to reach out to me for an assessment of your family's current situation. One call may save your family thousands of dollars.

Dan Evertsz, CEO
College Money Pros
Dan@collegemoneypros.com
www.collegemoneypros.com

ABOUT DAN EVERTSZ

Dan Evertsz is the CEO of College Money Pros located in San Ramon, California. Dan is considered one of the premier national experts in the College Planning and Funding arena. Dan has appeared in numerous press articles as well as many radio and television interviews. His firm has helped over 1,000 families lower the out-of-pocket costs of a college education.

Dan has been featured in many press publications (MSNBC, US News & World Report, LA Weekly, and the Sacramento Bee) and has done many radio and television appearances. Dan is active in his church and community. Dan is married to his lovely wife, Deborah, for 28 years and has two children, Ashlee, a recent graduate of NYU's highly acclaimed graduate occupational therapist program and his son, Khari, who is a recent high school graduate.

This book is proudly published by WIPublish, A Division of Women Ignite International.

WIPublish

Contact: Terilee Harrison, Director WIPublish
terilee@womenigniteinternational.com

Find us online: www.womenigniteinternational.com
LIKE us on Facebook: www.Facebook.com/wipublish

Made in United States
North Haven, CT
04 November 2026

21772049R00044